To *Heather*

on the occasion of *your*

Confirmation

Date **11th May, 1997**

This edition copyright © 1995 Lion Publishing
Illustrations copyright © 1995 Simon Bull

Published by
Lion Publishing plc
Sandy Lane West, Oxford, England
ISBN 0 7459 3361 0
Albatross Books Pty Ltd
PO Box 320, Sutherland, NSW 2232, Australia
ISBN 0 7324 1323 0

First edition 1995
10 9 8 7 6 5 4 3 2 1 0

A catalogue record for this book is available
from the British Library

Printed and bound in Singapore

A Faith to Live By

THE EARLIEST CHRISTIAN CREED
AND ITS MEANING

LION
Giftlines

Introduction

From the very beginning of Christianity, followers of Jesus Christ were people who believed certain things. Those beliefs were gradually formed into what is called a 'creed' (*Credo* is the Latin for 'I believe'). These beliefs became an important test of true Christianity. Today, all over the world, creeds are used by Christians as a statement of their faith.

Creeds were in use from the earliest stage of the Christian Church. At first they were in question-and-answer form for use at baptism. The person wishing to be baptized as a Christian would be asked such questions as, 'Do you believe in God, the Father almighty?' The candidate would respond, 'I believe.'

The series of questions were added to gradually, covering essential aspects of the Christian faith. The Apostles' Creed grew out of these early beginnings around the middle of the fourth century. It was called the Apostles' Creed as it summarized the teaching of the leaders of the early Church. It is often used today in Christian worship as a declaration of faith.

In this book the beliefs enshrined in the Apostles' creed are traced to their Biblical origins to show how the early Christians came to believe what they believed. The aim is to gain a clear grasp of the faith as a basis for discipleship today.

The Apostles' Creed

I believe in God, the Father almighty,
creator of heaven and earth.

I believe in Jesus Christ, his only Son,
    our Lord.
He was conceived by the power of the
    Holy Spirit
and born of the Virgin Mary.
He suffered under Pontius Pilate,
    was crucified, died, and was buried.
He descended to the dead.
On the third day he rose again.
He ascended into heaven,
    and is seated at the right hand of
    the Father.
He will come again to judge the living
    and the dead.

I believe in the Holy Spirit,
the holy catholic Church,
the communion of saints,
the forgiveness of sins,
the resurrection of the body,
and the life everlasting. Amen.

Christians Believe...

**IN GOD,
THE FATHER ALMIGHTY,
CREATOR OF HEAVEN
AND EARTH**

The Bible's starting point is the existence of God. It is not discussed or argued, it is simply a given. God is. The first stories in the book of Genesis reveal God to be a creator. The being who, from his own imagination and power, brought the universe into being. The sheer scale of this claim leads to the belief that God is almighty. But he is also seen as more than that. The picture language of a father is used to show that he is not remote, but that he cares intimately for the world he has made.

1 CORINTHIANS 8:6

There is for us only one God, the Father, who is the Creator of all things and for whom we live.

PSALM 145:3

The Lord is great and is to be highly praised; his greatness is beyond understanding.

REVELATION 1:8

'I am the first and the last,' says the Lord God Almighty, who is, who was, and who is to come.

GENESIS 1:1–3

In the beginning, when God created the universe, the earth was formless and desolate. The raging ocean that covered everything was engulfed in total darkness, and the power of God was moving over the water. Then God commanded, 'Let there be light' — and light appeared.

IN JESUS CHRIST, GOD'S ONLY SON, OUR LORD

Just as God's power is seen in creation, so his character is revealed in the man, Jesus Christ. Christians believe that Jesus was none other than God come to the earth as a person – the only way we would ever be able to understand what the invisible God is like. Again the picture language of a 'son' is used to describe the unique relationship between Jesus on earth and God is heaven – two equal persons in one God.

2 PETER 1:16–18

An early follower wrote: 'We have not depended on made-up stories in making known to you the mighty coming of our Lord Jesus Christ. With our own eyes we saw his greatness. We were there when he was given honour and glory by God the Father, when the voice came to him from the Supreme Glory, saying, "This is my own dear Son, with whom I am well pleased!" We ourselves heard this voice coming from heaven, when we were with him on the holy mountain.'

JOHN 10:30, 36–38

Jesus said: 'The Father and I are one. The Father chose me and sent me into the world. How, then, can you say that I blaspheme because I said that I am the Son of God? Do not believe me, then, if I am not doing the things my Father wants me to do. But if I do them, even though you do not believe me, you should at least believe my deeds, in order that you may know once and for all that the Father is in me and that I am in the Father.'

JESUS CHRIST WAS CONCEIVED BY THE POWER OF THE HOLY SPIRIT AND BORN OF THE VIRGIN MARY

This phrase introduces the third equal person in the one God, the Holy Spirit. He represents God's continuous presence on earth and his power to affect events in time and space. He acted to bring Jesus into the world through an ordinary girl, Mary of Nazareth. Jesus' supernatural conception marked the beginning of his unique life as God and man, fully human yet fully divine. The word we use for this event is 'incarnation' which means to 'take flesh'.

MATTHEW 1:18–25

This was how the birth of Jesus Christ took place. His mother Mary was engaged to Joseph, but before they were married, she found out that she was going to have a baby by the Holy Spirit. Joseph was a man who always did what was right, but he did not want to disgrace Mary publicly; so he made plans to break the engagement privately.

While he was thinking about this, an angel of the Lord appeared to him in a dream and said, 'Joseph, descendant of David, do not be afraid to take Mary to be your wife. For it is by the Holy Spirit that she has conceived. She will have a son, and you will name him Jesus – because he will save his people from their sins.'

... So when Joseph woke up, he married Mary, as the angel of the Lord had told him to. But he had no sexual relations with her before she gave birth to her son. And Joseph named him Jesus.

JESUS CHRIST SUFFERED UNDER PONTIUS PILATE, WAS CRUCIFIED, DIED, AND WAS BURIED

Jesus' whole life on earth is taken as read here, because the events of his death and resurrection are so important to the Christian faith. Jesus' death was for a purpose and all the events of his life led towards it. The earliest Christians were keen to emphasize the historical fact of Jesus' death, because his resurrection was so amazing that people doubted he had actually died.

LUKE 23:13–25, 32–34, 44–46

Pilate [the Roman governor of Judea], called together the chief priests, the leaders, and the people, and said to them, 'You brought this man to me and said that he was misleading the people. Now, I have examined him here in your presence, and I have not found him guilty of any of the crimes you accuse him of ... There is nothing this man has done to deserve death. So I will have him whipped and let him go.'

The whole crowd cried out, 'Kill him! Set Barabbas free for us!' (Barabbas had been put in prison for a riot that had taken place in the city, and for murder.) Pilate wanted to set Jesus free, so he appealed to the crowd again ... but they kept on shouting at the top of their voices that Jesus should be crucified, and finally their shouting succeeded. So Pilate passed the sentence on Jesus that they were asking for. He set free the man they wanted, the one who had been put in prison for riot and murder, and he handed Jesus over for them to do as they wished.

Two other men, both of them criminals, were also led out to be put to death with Jesus. When they came to the place called 'The Skull', they crucified Jesus there, and the two criminals, one on his right and the other on his left. Jesus said, 'Forgive them, Father! They don't know what they are doing.'

It was about twelve o'clock when the sun stopped shining and darkness covered the whole country until three o'clock; and the curtain hanging in the Temple was torn in two. Jesus cried out in a loud voice, 'Father! In your hands I place my spirit!' He said this and died.

MATTHEW 27:57–60

When it was evening, a rich man from Arimathea arrived; his name was Joseph, and he also was a disciple of Jesus. He went into the presence of Pilate and asked for the body of Jesus. Pilate gave orders for the body to be given to Joseph. So Joseph took it, wrapped it in a new linen sheet, and placed it in his own tomb, which he had just recently dug out of solid rock. Then he rolled a large stone across the entrance to the tomb and went away.

JESUS CHRIST DESCENDED
TO THE DEAD

Jesus was physically dead for the three days between the crucifixion and the resurrection. Of course we have no knowledge of what happens to those who die, but we believe that Jesus also experienced something of that state during his three days in the tomb.

MATTHEW 12:38–40

Some time before Jesus' death: Some teachers of the Law and some Pharisees spoke up. 'Teacher,' they said, 'we want to see you perform a miracle.' 'How evil and godless are the people of this day!' Jesus exclaimed. 'You ask me for a miracle? No! The only miracle you will be given is the miracle of the prophet Jonah. In the same way that Jonah spent three days and nights in the big fish, so will the Son of Man spend three days and nights in the depths of the earth.'

1 PETER 3:18–19

Christ died for sins once and for all, a good man on behalf of sinners, in order to lead you to God. He was put to death physically, but made alive spiritually, and in his spiritual existence he went and preached to the imprisoned spirits.

JESUS CHRIST ROSE AGAIN ON THE THIRD DAY

This is the crucial historical event upon which Christianity is founded. Before Jesus' amazing first words to Mary outside the tomb, the disciples were a defeated, frightened group of deserted followers. Then everything fell into place. Jesus had conquered death and was alive for ever. Everything he had taught them was true.

MATTHEW 27:62–66

The chief priests and the Pharisees met with Pilate and said, 'Sir, we remember that while that liar was still alive he said, "I will be raised to life three days later." Give orders, then, for his tomb to be carefully guarded until the third day, so that his disciples will not be able to go and steal the body, and then tell the people that he was raised from death. This last lie would be even worse than the first one.' 'Take a guard,' Pilate told them; 'go and make the tomb as secure as you can.' So they left and made the tomb secure by putting a seal on the stone and leaving the guard on watch.

MATTHEW 28:1–9

After the Sabbath, as Sunday morning was dawning, Mary Magdalene and the other Mary went to look at the tomb. Suddenly there was a violent earthquake; an angel of the Lord came down from heaven, rolled the stone away, and sat on it. His appearance was like lightning, and his clothes were white as snow. The guards were so afraid that they trembled and became like dead men.

The angel spoke to the women. 'You must not be afraid,' he said. 'I know you are looking for Jesus, who was crucified. He is not here; he has been raised, just as he said. Come here and see the place where he was lying. Go quickly now, and tell his disciples, "He has been raised from death, and now he is going to Galilee ahead of you; there you will see him!" Remember what I have told you.'

So they left the tomb in a hurry, afraid and yet filled with joy, and ran to tell his disciples. Suddenly Jesus met them and said, 'Peace be with you.' They came up to him, took hold of his feet, and worshipped him. 'Do not be afraid,' Jesus said to them. 'Go and tell my brothers to go to Galilee, and there they will see me.'

LUKE 24:44–47

When Jesus appeared to his disciples he said: 'These are the very things I told you about while I was still with you: everything written about me in the Law of Moses, the writings of the prophets, and the Psalms had to come true.' Then he opened their minds to understand the Scriptures, and said to them, 'This is what is written: the Messiah must suffer and must rise from death three days later, and in his name the message about repentance and the forgiveness of sins must be preached to all nations.'

JESUS CHRIST ASCENDED INTO HEAVEN, AND IS SEATED AT THE RIGHT HAND OF GOD THE FATHER

The first disciples were eye witnesses to the fact that Jesus left the earth in a miraculous way. One minute he was with them on the mountain. The next he was gone. The phrase 'seated at the right hand' is picture language to express the position of honour given to Jesus because of his unique relationship with the Father.

JOHN 20:17

Jesus said to Mary after his resurrection: 'Do not hold on to me . . . because I have not yet gone back up to the Father. But go to my brothers and tell them that I am returning to him who is my Father and their Father, my God and their God.'

LUKE 24:49–51

Again, after his resurrection, Jesus said to his disciples: 'I myself will send upon you what my Father has promised. But you must wait in the city until the power from above comes down upon you.' Then he led them out of the city as far as Bethany, where he raised his hands and blessed them. As he was blessing them, he departed from them and was taken up into heaven.

HEBREWS 12:2

Let us keep our eyes fixed on Jesus, on whom our faith depends from beginning to end. He did not give up because of the cross! On the contrary, because of the joy that was waiting for him, he thought nothing of the disgrace of dying on the cross, and he is now seated at the right-hand side of God's throne.

JESUS CHRIST WILL COME AGAIN TO JUDGE THE LIVING AND THE DEAD

Jesus often used picture language when he spoke about his return to this earth because it is not easy for us to grasp. We do not know exactly how it will come about, neither do we know when it will be. However, Christians believe that Jesus will one day come to wind up history as we know it and to dispense true justice at last. It is something to look forward to, but it is also a challenge to the way we live now.

MATTHEW 24:27, 36   **Jesus said:** 'The Son of Man will come like the lightning which flashes across the whole sky from the east to the west. No one knows, however, when that day and hour will come—neither the angels in heaven nor the Son; the Father alone knows.'

JOHN 14:1–3   **Jesus said:** 'Do not be worried and upset... Believe in God and believe also in me. There are many rooms in my Father's house, and I am going to prepare a place for you. I would not tell you this if it were not so. And after I go and prepare a place for you, I will come back and take you to myself, so that you will be where I am.'

Christians Believe...

IN THE HOLY SPIRIT

It is God's Spirit – the Holy Spirit – who gives new spiritual life to everyone who becomes a Christian. He comes to live in us and to help us live in a way that pleases God.

JOHN 14:16–18

Jesus said: 'I will ask the Father, and he will give you another Helper, who will stay with you for ever. He is the Spirit who reveals the truth about God. The world cannot receive him, because it cannot see him or know him. But you know him, because he remains with you and is in you. When I go, you will not be left all alone; I will come back to you.'

GALATIANS 5:22–23, 25

The Spirit produces love, joy, peace, patience, kindness, goodness, faithfulness, humility, and self-control. The Spirit has given us life; he must also control our lives.

EPHESIANS 4:30–32

Do not make God's Holy Spirit sad; for the Spirit is God's mark of ownership on you, a guarantee that the Day will come when God will set you free.

Get rid of all bitterness, passion, and anger. No more shouting or insults, no more hateful feelings of any sort. Instead, be kind and tender-hearted to one another, and forgive one another, as God has forgiven you through Christ.

This phrase has nothing to do with denominations. The word 'catholic' comes from the Greek *katholikos* meaning 'general'. It describes the universal Church which consists of all Christian believers everywhere.

EPHESIANS 1:22–23 God put all things under Christ's feet and gave him to the church as supreme Lord over all things. The church is Christ's body, the completion of him who himself completes all things everywhere.

GALATIANS 3:26–28 It is through faith that all of you are God's children in union with Christ Jesus. You were baptized into union with Christ, and now you are clothed, so to speak, with the life of Christ himself. So there is no difference between Jews and Gentiles, between slaves and free, between men and women; you are all one in union with Christ Jesus.

Christians Believe...

IN THE COMMUNION OF SAINTS

The word 'saint' in the Bible is used to describe each person who belongs to God. Christians recognise that they are part of one large family and that they enjoy a special relationship with all other Christian believers.

ACTS 2:42–47

The very first Christians spent their time in learning from the apostles, taking part in the fellowship, and sharing in the fellowship meals and the prayers. Many miracles and wonders were being done through the apostles, and everyone was filled with awe. All the believers continued together in close fellowship and shared their belongings with one another. They would sell their property and possessions, and distribute the money among all, according to what each one needed. Day after day they met as a group in the Temple, and they had their meals together in their homes, eating with glad and humble hearts, praising God, and enjoying the good will of all the people. And every day the Lord added to their group those who were being saved.

GALATIANS 6:2, 10

Help to carry one another's burdens, and in this way you will obey the law of Christ. So then, as often as we have the chance, we should do good to everyone, and especially to those who belong to our family in the faith.

Forgiveness is the wonderful gift at the heart of Christianity. Everyone needs to find forgiveness for the things that they have done wrong and the ways in which they have fallen short of God's high standards. In an amazing way, God's son took the punishment for our shortcomings – our sins – on himself when he died on the cross and we can be forgiven in his name.

1 JOHN 4:9–10

God showed his love for us by sending his only Son into the world, so that we might have life through him. This is what love is: it is not that we have loved God, but that he loved us and sent his Son to be the means by which our sins are forgiven.

ROMANS 5:6–10

When we were still helpless, Christ died for the wicked at the time that God chose. It is a difficult thing for someone to die for a righteous person. It may even be that someone might dare to die for a good person. But God has shown how much he loves us – it was while we were still sinners that Christ died for us! By his sacrificial death we are now put right with God; how much more, then, will we be saved by him from God's anger! We were God's enemies, but he made us his friends through the death of his Son.

Jesus' resurrection body was different. He was recognisable and people could touch him. But he could also appear and disappear at will. There was something familiar but also something totally new about him. In the same way, Christians believe that they will be given new, perfect bodies for the new life of heaven.

JOHN 6: 39–40, 44

Jesus said: 'It is the will of him who sent me that I should not lose any of all those he had given me, but that I should raise them all to life on the last day. For what my Father wants is that all who see the Son and believe in him should have eternal life. And I will raise them to life on the last day. No one can come to me unless the Father who sent me draws him to me; and I will raise him to life on the last day.'

JOHN 5:28–29

'Do not be surprised at this; the time is coming when all the dead will hear his voice and come out of their graves: those who have done good will rise and live, and those who have done evil will rise and be condemned.'

PHILIPPIANS 3:20–21

We ... are citizens of heaven, and we eagerly wait for our Saviour, the Lord Jesus Christ, to come from heaven. He will change our weak mortal bodies and make them like his own glorious body, using that power by which he is able to bring all things under his rule.

PHILIPPIANS 2:5–11   Christ Jesus ... always had the nature of God,
... of his own free will he gave up all he had,
     and took the nature of a servant.
He became like man
     and appeared in human likeness.
He was humble and walked the path
     of obedience all the way to death—
his death on the cross.
For this reason God raised him
     to the highest place above
and gave him the name that is greater
     than any other name.
And so, in honour of the name of Jesus
     all beings in heaven, on earth, and
in the world below
     will fall on their knees,
and all will openly proclaim that Jesus
     Christ is Lord,
to the glory of God the Father.

Be thou my vision, O Lord of my heart,
be all else but naught to me, save that thou art;
be thou my best thought in the day and the night,
both waking and sleeping, thy presence my light.

Be thou my wisdom, be thou my true word,
be thou ever with me, and I with thee, Lord;
be thou my great Father, and I thy true son;
be thou in me dwelling, and I with thee one.

Be thou my breastplate, my sword for the fight;
be thou my whole armour, be thou my true might;
be thou my soul's shelter, be thou my strong tower:
O raise thou me heavenward, great Power
   of my power.

Riches I heed not, nor man's empty praise;
be thou mine inheritance now and always;
be thou and thou only the first in my heart;
O Sovereign of heaven, my treasure thou art.

High King of heaven, thou heaven's bright Sun,
O grant me its joys after vict'ry is won;
great Heart of my own heart, whatever befall,
still be thou my vision, thou Ruler of all.

8TH CENTURY IRISH, TRANSLATED BY MARY BYRNE (1880–1931)
VERSIFIED BY ELEANOR HULL (1860–1935)

O God, the living God,
who has put your own eternity in our
hearts, and has made us to hunger and
thirst after you: satisfy, we pray, the
instricts which you have implanted in us,
that we may find you in life and life in
you; through Jesus Christ our Lord.
Amen.

To him who sits on the throne
and to the Lamb,
be praise and honour, glory and might,
for ever and ever!

FROM THE BOOK OF REVELATION

Christians Believe...

Because God's Spirit lives in us, Christians already experience a new quality of life. But death is seen as the way into a new dimension of living, totally outside the narrow restrictions of time and space. We will still be ourselves but we will be living the new life of heaven with all its infinite possibilities. We will be alive with God for ever.

JOHN 11:25

Jesus said: 'I am the resurrection and the life. Whoever believes in me will live, even though he dies; and whoever lives and believes in me will never die.'

1 JOHN 5:11–13

God has given us eternal life, and this life has its source in his Son. Whoever has the Son has this life; whoever does not have the Son of God does not have life. I am writing this to you so that you may know that you have eternal life – you that believe in the Son of God.

REVELATION 21:1, 3–4

Then I saw a new heaven and a new earth. The first heaven and the first earth disappeared, and the sea vanished. I heard a loud voice speaking from the throne: 'Now God's home is with mankind! He will live with them, and they shall be his people. God himself will be with them, and he will be their God. He will wipe away all tears from their eyes. There will be no more death, no more grief or crying or pain. The old things have disappeared.'

Christianity is Jesus Christ

Christianity is based on a relationship with God as a person. It involves a personal commitment to Jesus Christ. Christianity begins with God's initiative – the incarnation – God becoming man. Christians believe that, as perfect God and perfect man, Jesus Christ is the link to bring God and people together.

JOHN 14:6

Jesus said: 'I am the way, the truth, and the life; no one goes to the Father except by me.'

1 TIMOTHY 3:16

No one can deny how great is the secret
  of our religion:
He appeared in human form,
  was shown to be right by the Spirit,
  and was seen by the angels.
He was preached among the nations,
  was believed in throughout the world,
  and was taken up to heaven.